INSIDE THE WORLD OF MATTER

Jane Weir, MPhys

Physical Science Readers:
Inside the World of Matter

Publishing Credits

Editorial Director
Dona Herweck Rice

Creative Director
Lee Aucoin

Associate Editor
Joshua BishopRoby

Illustration Manager
Timothy J. Bradley

Editor-in-Chief
Sharon Coan, M.S.Ed.

Publisher
Rachelle Cracchiolo, M.S.Ed.

Science Contributor
Sally Ride Science

Science Consultants
Michael E. Kopecky,
   Science Department Chair,
   Chino Hills High School
Jane Weir, MPhys

Teacher Created Materials Publishing
5301 Oceanus Drive
Huntington Beach, CA 92649-1030
http://www.tcmpub.com
ISBN 978-0-7439-0567-1
© 2007 Teacher Created Materials Publishing
Reprinted 2011
BP 5028

Table of Contents

The Matter with Matter

Think of everything in your house. Think of how different these things are to each other. Some are shiny, some are dull. Some are soft, some are hard. Some are magnetic, some aren't. Some are cold to the touch, some aren't. Some are brittle, some are bouncy. Some are solid, some are liquid, and some are gas. Some you can see, some you don't even notice. Some are alive, some have never lived. Some are good to eat, some are poisonous.

Now, think of everything in your hometown, your country, the world, and even the universe. There are millions of different types of things in the universe. All of them are made of **matter**.

Matter is the substance, or stuff, that makes up everything. But what makes up matter? Amazingly, of all the millions of things in the universe, every single last one of them is made up of just over 100 different ingredients. The proper word for these ingredients is **elements** (EL-uh-ments).

In this book, you will learn more about the ingredients that make up all the stuff in the universe.

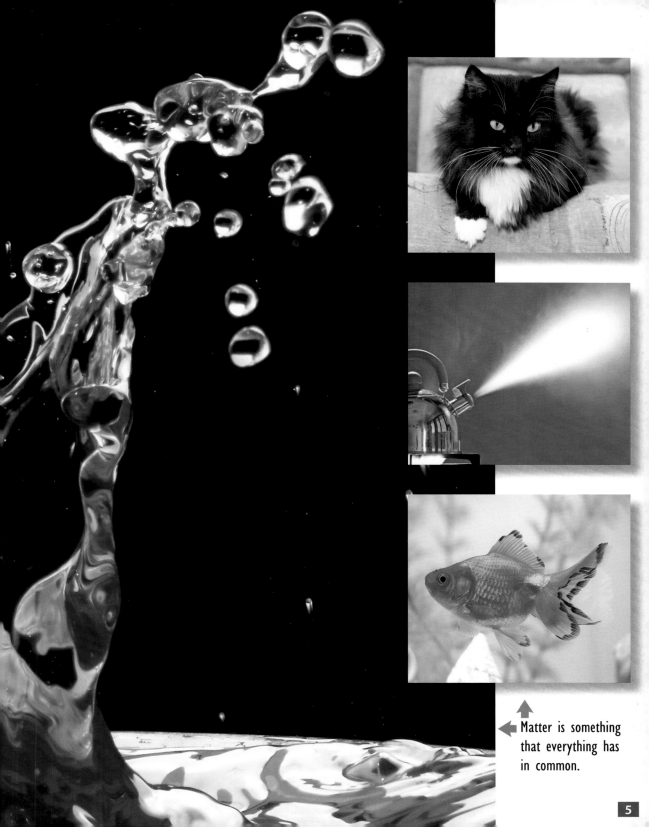

Matter is something
that everything has
in common.

All matter is made from **atoms**. Atoms are tiny **particles** (PAR-tuh-kuhls). Even the air is made of atoms. Atoms are so small that a million billion billion of them fit on a teaspoon. No person can see them without help. It takes a powerful microscope to get a good look.

There are about 100 different types of atoms. They can be put together in many ways. Each way makes one of the millions of different things that exist. This is called **atomic arrangement** (uh-TOM-ik-uh-RANGE-muhnt).

Things that are made of just one type of atom are called elements. There are about 100 different elements.

Helium atom   Hydrogen atom

Fun Fact

Atoms are so small that it would take about 1,000 years to count all the atoms in one single dot, like this period. The number of atoms in your body couldn't be counted in the time since the universe began!

36 million, 893 thousand, 224...

We Too Are Stardust

The universe started off as mostly hydrogen. All the other elements were formed in nuclear reactions in stars. When stars get old, some of them swell and explode. Different elements are scattered all over the universe. This provides the materials for making all the things we see on Earth, including us. The atoms in our bodies are no different from the atoms in anything else. It is the way they are arranged that makes us different from a can of soup or a comet's tail.

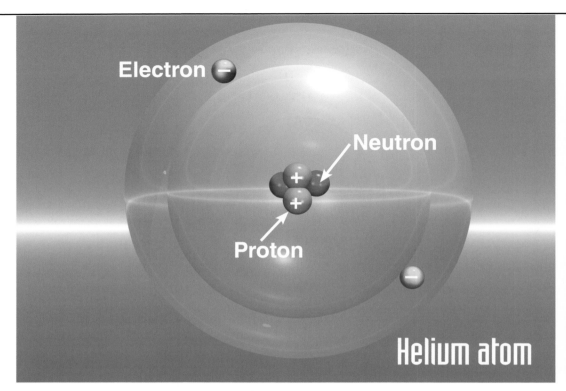

Electron −

Neutron

Proton

Helium atom

⬆ This diagram shows the balance of charge in a helium atom. The two positive protons balance the two negative electrons.

Inside Atoms

Each atom is made of even smaller parts. There are three basic types of these parts. They are **protons** (PROH-tons), **neutrons** (NOO-trons), and **electrons** (uh-LEK-trons). The protons and neutrons are crowded tightly together in the middle of the atom. This is called the **nucleus** (noo-CLEE-uhs). Outside of this grouping is an area of the atom that is mostly empty space. The tiny electrons zip around within this space. Electrons are even smaller than protons or neutrons. They travel very fast.

Protons have a positive electric charge. Neutrons have no charge. Electrons have a negative charge. There are always the same number of protons and electrons in an atom. Their charges balance each other. Most atoms have no charge. That's something like mixing black and white paint. You no longer have black or white. You have gray—no charge.

The thing that makes elements different is the number of protons in their atoms. Hydrogen atoms are the simplest type of atom. They have only one proton and one electron.

Electron

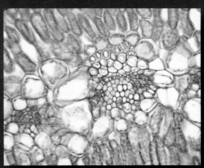

The Periodic Table

The elements can be grouped by their **properties**. Properties are what make each element unique. They include such things as number of electrons and distance between atoms. Elements can also be grouped by how **reactive** they are. That means how they act with one another. It also means how they react to heat and cold.

A good way to arrange the elements is in a table. In 1869, a Russian scientist made a table to organize the elements. It is called the **periodic** (peer-ee-OD-ik) **table**. It is a chart that scientists still use today.

The Stability of Elements

When a substance is made of all the same kind of atoms, it is called an element. Elements can't be changed easily into other elements. In other words, iron will always be iron. It can't be changed into any other element. You can heat it. You can hit it. You can drop it in acid. No matter what you do, it will still be iron. It might not look the same after doing any of these things. But it will still be made of iron atoms.

The reason is simple. To change one element into another means changing the nucleus of each atom. It is very hard to break apart a nucleus. It is held together by a very strong force.

Fun Fact

In ancient times, people believed they could make gold. They thought that heating common metals with other elements would do it. Nowadays, we know this isn't true. An element can't be changed by heat.

Molecules

Atoms can join to make **molecules** (MOL-uh-kyools). In molecules, atoms share some of their electrons.

Molecules join to form substances. Each molecule of a substance has the same properties as the whole. That means that one molecule of a substance reacts in the same way as a whole group of them.

Some elements exist as molecules. An example of this is oxygen. Oxygen is in the air we breathe. It is made up of two oxygen atoms bonded together. It can be written as O_2.

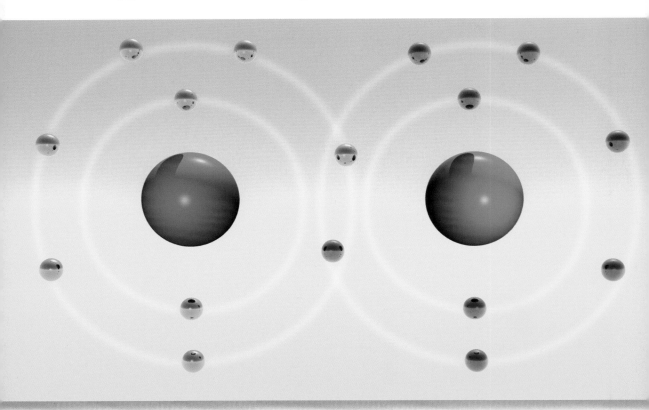

These are two oxygen atoms bonded together by the sharing of their electrons.

Why Do Snowflakes Have Six Sides?

When molecules join to one another, they do it in patterns. The patterns they make depend on how the parts that make them are attracted to one another. The shape of the molecules and their tiny bonds decide what patterns we see. When water freezes, each molecule makes six bonds to other water molecules. That's why snowflakes have six sides.

Many patterns in nature happen because of the shapes molecules make when they bond. For example, leaf veins are made in this way.

Ice crystals freeze together in intricate six-sided shapes. We call them snowflakes!

Compounds

A **compound** is made when the atoms of different elements join together. They become a new substance. The compound has different properties than the elements that make it.

For example, water is made from hydrogen and oxygen. But it isn't like either of them. Water is a compound. Each water molecule has two kinds of atoms. There are two hydrogen and one oxygen atom. This is written as H_2O. The number two means that there are two hydrogen atoms in the molecule. No number after the O means there is just one atom of oxygen.

Compounds are made by reactive (ree-AK-tiv) elements. Reactive elements join easily with others. Some elements are very reactive and some are not. The more reactive an element, the more likely it will form compounds.

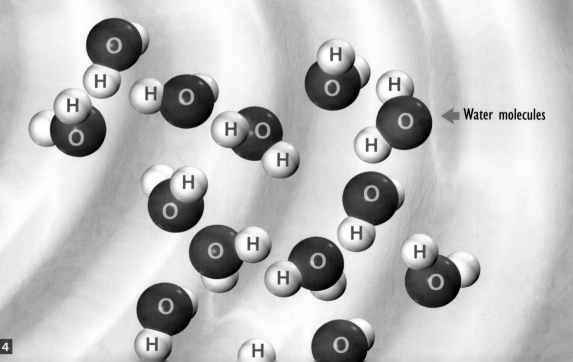

← Water molecules

Amazing!

There are about 1,000,000,000, 000,000,000,000,000 (one septillion) water molecules in one medium-size glass of water.

Too Hot to Handle

A very unreactive element is argon gas. It is used in light bulbs because it won't catch fire when hot. A very reactive element is sodium metal. It needs to be kept in oil because if it touches air, it can catch fire!

States of Matter

Matter can exist as a solid, liquid, or gas. These are the **states of matter**. When water is solid, you can skate on it. You can put it in your drinks to make them cold. We call this ice. When water is a liquid, you can swim in it. You can drink it or take a shower. You can water plants with it. You can fill your dog's water bowl with it. When water is a gas, it is called water vapor or steam. Water vapor would never stay in your dog's water bowl. It is what clouds are made of. You see it as steam from a kettle or rising off a bowl of hot soup.

▲ Icebergs are like ice cubes floating in a glass of water. They float in the ocean. Just like ice cubes, they rise to the surface.

Why Does Water Appear Outside My Glass?

On a hot humid day, the air contains many water molecules. These molecules have a lot of energy and move around a great deal. If they hit the sides of a cold glass of water, then they lose some of their energy and slow down. Some of the molecules slow down so much that they don't have enough energy to be in a gas any more. They turn into liquid on the outside of the glass.

Substances can change from one state of matter to another. For example, they may melt or **evaporate** (uh-VAP-uh-rate). However, changing state won't change the molecules. They stay the same. Water molecules are the same whether they are ice, water, or vapor.

Most substances expand when they heat up. This is because the molecules vibrate more and push away from each other. The amount molecules move is different for solids, liquids, and gases. The most active molecules are in gases. They are also the farthest apart. The least active are in solids. They are often the closest together.

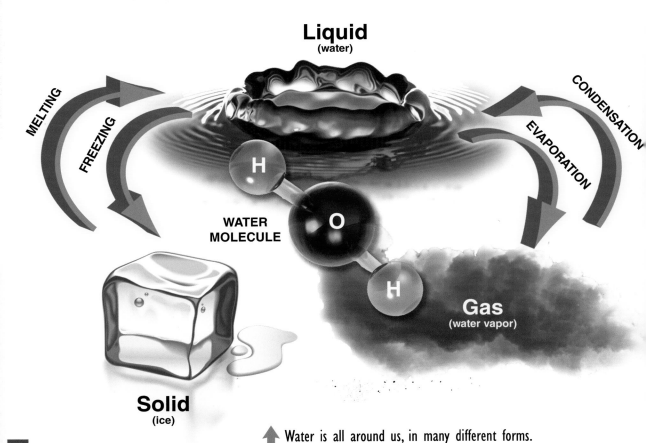

Water is all around us, in many different forms.

Try It!

Most elements contract (get smaller) when they freeze. This is because molecules in solids move less than in liquids. Water is one of the few elements that expands when frozen. Because ice is less dense than water, it floats. If you put a full container of water in the freezer with a lid on it, the lid will pop off when it freezes.

Moving Windows

Glass is a solid but acts like a liquid over long periods of time. Some very old windows in buildings found in Europe are thicker at the bottom than at the top because the glass has "flowed" downward over time.

Ice cream is a solid. When it melts, it becomes a liquid.

Why Does Soup Cool Faster When I Blow on It?

The surface of a bowl of soup is not still. If we could magnify it millions of times, we would see a lot happening. The molecules are leaving and returning to the surface from the air just above it all the time. Bits are evaporating and condensing all the time. If you blow on the soup, then you remove the molecules that might have been bobbing about in the air above the soup. Instead of diving back in, they are blown away. So, more molecules leave than come back. The soup evaporates. The molecules that leave have more energy than the rest in the soup. So, when they leave, the ones left have less energy altogether. Energy in molecules is the same as heat. As the molecules with more energy leave, the soup cools down.

Molecules in a solid are packed together closely. They have fixed positions. They can only move by vibrating in these positions. That is why solids keep their shape. They don't flow. It is hard to compress (squish) solids because their molecules are already close together.

Molecules in a liquid are farther apart. They can move past each other easily. Liquids can flow and change shape. They can spread out to make puddles. A liquid will fill the bottom of any container it is in. It will still keep the same volume. It won't get any bigger.

Molecules in a gas are far apart compared with solids or liquids. They can move freely. A gas will fill all the space in a container. It is easy to compress a gas because the molecules are far apart.

Solid   Liquid   Gas

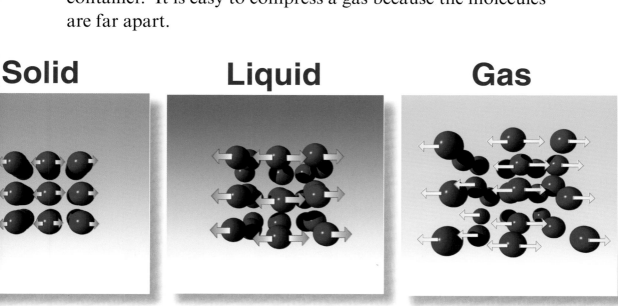

▲ A change from a solid to a liquid or a gas is marked by a change in the space between molecules.

Why Can I Eat Sodium Chloride but not Sodium or Chlorine?

The chemical name for salt is sodium chloride. Each salt molecule is made from one atom of sodium and one atom of chlorine. Scientists write it as *NaCl*. *Na* stands for sodium. *Cl* stands for chlorine. On its own, sodium is a metal that you wouldn't want to eat. Chlorine is a poisonous gas. But together, they make salt. Salt is not a metal, and it is not poisonous. Luckily, when things join together in reactions, the substances they make are new. They have different properties than the things they are made of. For example, rust is made of iron and oxygen. However, it doesn't behave like either of them.

When you cool something, you take energy from it. The colder it is, the less its atoms move. At minus 273 degrees Celsius (SEL-see-uhs), it is very cold. It is so cold that nearly everything will be a solid. Molecules will vibrate as little as possible. This is the coldest anything can get. It is called **absolute** (AB-suh-loot) **zero**. No more energy can be removed from something at absolute zero.

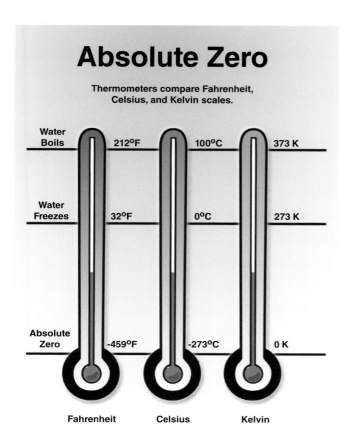

Absolute Zero

Thermometers compare Fahrenheit, Celsius, and Kelvin scales.

	Fahrenheit	Celsius	Kelvin
Water Boils	212°F	100°C	373 K
Water Freezes	32°F	0°C	273 K
Absolute Zero	-459°F	-273°C	0 K

Atoms normally bop around at 1,000 mph. Close to absolute zero, it's like they're moving in thick mud. While their movements normally seem random, near absolute zero their movements seem like a dance of tiny waves.

Max Planck
Thermodynamics is the study of heat and how it moves. The laws of thermodynamics describe why reactions happen. The conservation of energy, or keeping energy, is one of these laws. Max Planck, a famous scientist, studied this. He learned a lot about heat and energy. His work changed what scientists thought they knew.

Mixtures

A mixture is not the same as a compound. Some everyday mixtures are air and blood. They contain many different types of atoms and molecules. Not all of the atoms and molecules are joined through reactions. They can be separated easily if you know how.

The way to separate a mixture is to use the properties of the substances in the mixture. These properties are things such as the melting and boiling points. The ability to dissolve in water or oil is also a property. Another is whether or not it is magnetic. And one more property is the size of its solid chunks.

This diagram shows the parts that make up blood. The background photo shows red blood cells as seen through a microscope.

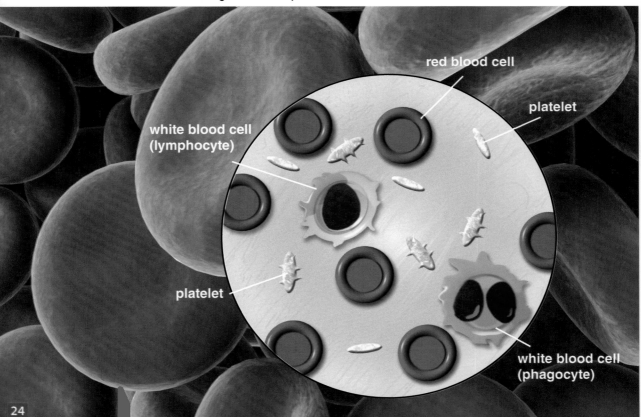

red blood cell

platelet

white blood cell (lymphocyte)

platelet

white blood cell (phagocyte)

What Makes a Lava Lamp Work?

A lava lamp is a light that glows in a bright color and shows a moving, changing mass inside it. The lamp works by using physical properties. It holds a mixture of water and wax. The wax is less dense than water when it is warm and melted. But it is denser than water when it is cold. When the lava lamp is turned on, a heater at the bottom warms the wax and softens it. As the wax softens, it gets less dense and floats to the top of the lamp in blobs. When it cools, it becomes solid and falls back down.

Separating Mixtures

If a solid can't be dissolved, filters can separate it from a liquid. For example, a coffee filter can separate coffee grounds from coffee. It can also filter solids from the air. A dust mask is used for that.

If a solid can be dissolved, boiling is one way to separate it from a liquid. For example, boiling sea water evaporates the water and leaves the salt crystals behind.

A screen can separate large solid particles from small solid particles. This can be done with pebbles in soil.

◄ Mixtures can be separated into their parts by filtering, evaporation, or other means.

Chromatography (kroh-muh-TOG-ruh-fee) separates substances in a mixture. It lets the different parts spread out from each other. For example, it can separate the dyes in ink. Scientists use it at crime scenes. They can use it to identify unknown substances such as blood.

A scientist is using paper chromatography to study dyes. This involves placing a small amount of the substance on a piece of filter paper, then slowly dripping a solvent (a substance that can dissolve another one) into the center of the paper. The solvent then spreads the substance out at differing rates. The distance traveled over time is used to identify each component.

Lab: *Separating Mixtures*

Scientists who study physics need to know all about matter. They need to know what it is made of and how it behaves. One important thing to know is how different substances act when together. Sometimes they join, as when hydrogen and oxygen make water. Other times, they simply mix. What is mixed can also be unmixed. This lab will help you to learn how to separate mixtures. You will need to know some laws of physics in order to do it.

Materials

- mixture of pebbles, sand, salt, and iron filings
- sieve with 1 cm holes
- filter paper
- filter funnel
- spoon
- two large beakers
- strong magnet
- tripod
- gauze
- tongs
- water

Procedure

1 Mix the pebbles, sand, salt, and iron filings.

2 Now, you will separate them again. In order to do it, you will need to use what you have learned and know about mixtures, their properties, and how to separate them.

Think about what you know about the materials in the mixture. Think about their properties. How can you separate them? Follow these remaining steps:

3 Sift out the pebbles using the sieve.

4 Use the magnet to remove the iron filings.

5 Put the sand and salt mixture into the large beaker. Add water and stir until all the salt is dissolved.

6 Put the filter paper inside the filter funnel. Stand a second large beaker below the funnel spout. Pour the mixture through the funnel. The sand will be left in the paper.

7 Leave the remaining mixture in a very warm or hot place until it evaporates.

If you follow these steps, you should be able to separate all the materials by using their physical properties.

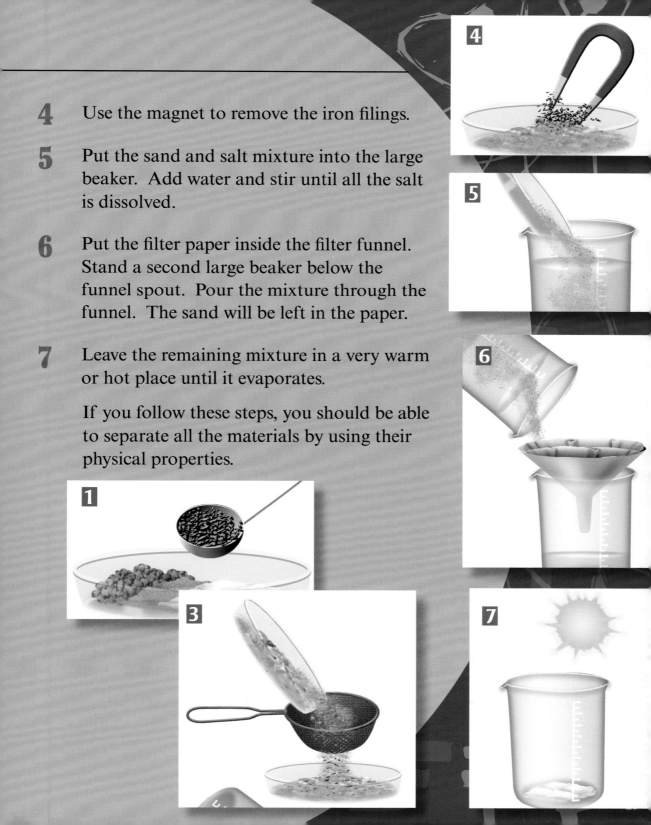

Glossary

absolute zero—the coldest temperature that anything can possibly get and at which all energy is removed from it

atom—the smallest particle of an element; it contains protons, neutrons, and electrons, and makes up all matter

atomic arrangement—the way atoms are arranged

chromatography—process for separating mixtures of substances with different boiling points or solubility

compound—substance made up of two or more different types of atoms joined together by chemical bonds

electron—small particle with a negative charge that travels fast around an atom

element—substance that is composed of just one type of atom and cannot be reduced to simpler substances by normal chemical means

evaporate—to change from a liquid state of matter to a gas

matter—something that has mass and exists in a solid, liquid, or gas

molecule—the smallest particle of a substance that retains its properties

neutron—particle with no charge found inside the nucleus of an atom

nucleus—the small, dense part in the middle of an atom, containing protons and neutrons

particle—a very small part

periodic table—a table showing all of the elements and how they are grouped

properties—qualities that make each element unique

proton—particle with a positive charge found inside the nucleus of an atom

reactive—a substance that easily combines with other substances in chemical reactions

state of matter—one of three forms that matter can take, either liquid, gas, or solid

Index

Sally Ride Science

Sally Ride Science™ is an innovative content company dedicated to fueling young people's interests in science. Our publications and programs provide opportunities for students and teachers to explore the captivating world of science—from astrobiology to zoology. We bring science to life and show young people that science is creative, collaborative, fascinating, and fun.